DISCOVER THE SEASONS

*To my husband, Doug Iverson, who has devoted
his entire career to teaching children the love of reading.
To our children and grandchildren: Michele, Kristin, Vanessa, Tyler,
Victoria, Aaron and Brycen.*

Published by DAWN Publications
12402 Bitney Springs Rd
Nevada City, CA 95959
880-545-7475
Email: nature@DawnPub.com
Website: www.DawnPub.com

Library of Congress Cataloging-in-Publication
(Prepared by Quality Books, Inc.)

Iverson, Diane.
Discover the seasons / Diane Iverson.
p. cm.
ISBN: 1-883220-43-2.

1. Seasons--Juvenile literature. I. Title.
QB637.4.I84 1996   508
QBI95-20659

Printed in China

10 9 8 7 6 5
First Edition

Designed by LeeAnn Brook Design
Type style is Caslon 540

DISCOVER
THE
SEASONS

Written and Illustrated by
Diane Iverson

DAWN Publications

A Letter to Parents and Teachers

In *Discover the Seasons* I hope to nurture a sense of wonder and curiosity in children, encouraging them to ask questions, explore, study and grow in harmony with creation.

Nature gives adults and children valuable opportunities to work, play and learn together–building relationships at the same time. Discovery and accomplishment are exciting things to share. Therefore, among the activities presented for ·ch season I have deliberately included ones that need adult involvement. The degree of difficulty of projects varies; there is something challenging for all elementary school children. Give more or less assistance as your child's age and skill level indicate.

The Resource section provides many book titles and addresses that will be of help to adults assisting with projects or teaching classes on related topics. As much as possible draw children into the research, teaching them the limitless resources available in books, libraries, their communities, and through the mail.

I hope that *Discover the Seasons* helps foster love of nature and reverence for beauty, and that you, dear reader, will play a part in healing creation. Happy reading!

—Diane Iverson

SPRING

Like jeweled ballerinas
who float on air
From bud to flower
so smartly,
Bright hummingbirds
dance with
elegant flair,
Announcing
nature's party!

Spring rain sends down its gentle showers,
Sweet perfume fills the air,
And falls on meadows of colorful flowers
With diamonds in their hair.

Spring is nature's birthday party. And what a party it is! Warm, soft rains bring life to plants that grow fresh new food for animals. The sweet fragrances of damp earth and colorful wildflowers fill the air. The earth is washed, decorated and ready to celebrate. Deer Mouse and Golden Mantled Ground Squirrel are happy to be among the honored guests.

Bold, curious creatures
begin their search
Of the warming, waking world,
And look for food
from a sunny perch
Where soft green
leaves uncurl.

After their long winter rest, animals are very active. They are hungry and eagerly eat new food as it grows. The Desert Tortoise comes out of his burrow to enjoy the sun. Birds like the Cactus Wren find insects to feed their growing babies in the nest.

In spring all nature
can gladly say
The world seems
young and strong.
Each beast declares
in its own special way,
The world has
been reborn!

Even the stream seems to lift its voice and sing,
"Celebrate!" Lush plants reach out with fluttering
green fingers to make a shady resting place for the
Black-tailed Deer and her fawn. Spring is a time for
peace and plenty. Spring brings hope for the future.

Things to do

Color Search

Explore your neighborhood, a park or a nature trail looking for as many spring colors as you can find. Colors must come from natural (not man-made) things. You will need a notebook, a piece of paper and a box of crayons or color markers. Mark each color on your paper, telling or drawing a picture of where you discovered it.

Bird Nests

In early spring, save dryer lint, cotton, short bits of string or yarn, and place them in a large open basket (a bicycle or egg basket will do). Hang the basket from a tree a few feet off the ground where it will be easy to watch from a window. Be patient and birds will come. How many can you name?

Wildflower Garden

Set aside a section of your yard or garden for wildflowers or native plants. A local nursery may be helpful in making plant and seed selections suitable for your area. See Resource section for mail-order sources for plants and seeds, wildflower gardening books and other items useful to the natural gardener. Ask your resource librarian for the address of state or local native plant societies that can help.

Prepare the soil, select seeds, plant, water, make plant labels and help with the regular care of your garden.

If you would like to attract butterflies or hummingbirds, consider these plants: Aster, Bee Plant, Cinquefoil, Clover, Columbine, Dandelion, Deervetch, Filaree, Gentian, Globemallow, Jewelweed, Lupine, Larkspur, Miner's Lettuce, Morning-glory, Penstemon, Sunflower, Violet, Wild Rose and Yucca. Enjoy your garden and watch for wild visitors.

Map Your Garden

Try making a map of your garden, drawing one inch for each foot of ground. For instance, if your garden is six feet by ten feet, your map will be six inches by ten inches. Draw all of the plants as they might look if you flew over your garden like a bird. Include any other things in the garden, like fences, a water faucet, path, bird bath, bird house, etc. Colored pencils are useful for drawing maps. Make small shapes as "symbols" of the things in your garden, and then make a "legend" in a corner of your map which explains what those symbols mean. For example, what symbol do you think you might use to show where you put a bird house, a bird bath or a bench?

Garden Labels   [Adult supervision required]

You can make attractive, reusable garden labels from recycled materials. To make two labels you will need: scissors, hammer, a large nail, a wire hanger that has a cardboard tube, two metal lids from large frozen juice containers, old seed packages, old flower catalogs, two 3" x 3" pieces of self-adhesive clear plastic and a glue stick.

• Use a hammer and nail to punch a hole near the edge of each lid. [Adults: pre-punch for younger children, and file any sharp edges with a metal file.]

• Select and cut out from catalogs or seed packages the names and pictures of flowers you will grow. Glue picture and name to lid so that nail hole is up. Use one picture and one name on each lid.

• When glue is dry, the pictures are ready to be covered with clear plastic. Trace a circle slightly smaller than juice lid on plastic backing. Cut out plastic so it fits over the picture but not over the nail hole. Peel backing with clean hands, and cover the picture.

• Cut the hanger with tin snips where the shoulder extensions meet at the hanger center. Discard hook and cardboard.

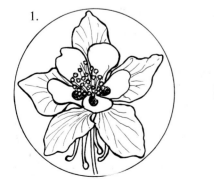

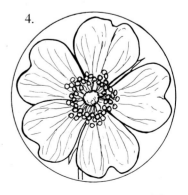

1.   2.   3.   4.

Copy and enlarge to 3-3/4" circles
for Spring Flower Mobile.

in the Spring...

- Slide nail hole in lid over hooked end of wire, and insert other end of wire in the ground in front of your plant. Your plant label is finished.

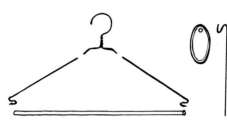

Recipe for Hummingbirds

[Adult supervision required]

Fill a hummingbird feeder with the following:
> Mix until dissolved: 1 cup boiling water and 1 cup white sugar
> Add 3 cups tap water.
> Stir well. Fill feeder.
> Refrigerate what is left in a clean, covered container.

Once the hummingbirds have discovered your feeder, you will probably need to fill it every day or two. Use a bird identification book (see Resources) to help you identify the birds that come to your feeder. Are they all hummingbirds?

Spring Flower Mobile [Adult supervision required]

- Materials needed: Colored pencils or fine-tipped felt markers, scissors, recycled cardboard, glue stick, hole punch or nail and hammer, two clothes hangers (wire and cardboard), tin snips, ruler, pencil, tape, about 4 yards of colored yarn.

- Make two enlarged photocopies of each of the four flower drawings on the opposite page.

- Color them, preferably using colored pencils or fine-tipped felt markers. What color should they be? If you want to be true to nature, look up their names in a flower identification book which will give you the color (see Resources). If you know the color but not the name, you can look it up that way too. The next time you see a wild flower, study its color, size and shape. Use that information to find it in the book and discover its name. To help you out, the names of three of the flowers, and just the color of the fourth, are printed upside down at the bottom of this page.

- Cut out the flower on the circle. Using the circle as a pattern, mark and cut four circles from thin recycled cardboard (department store clothing boxes work well).

- Attach flowers to both sides of cardboard circle with a glue stick.

- Use a hole punch or a large nail and hammer to make a hole 1/4" from edge of circle.

- Take the two wire hangers that have cardboard tubes and with tin snips cut off the handle of *one* of the hangers just above the twisted section.

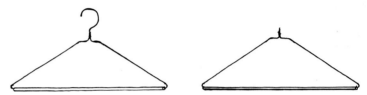

- Measure the length of each cardboard tube and mark the center with a pencil.

- Remove the wire from one end of the cardboard on the clipped hanger. Slip the cardboard from the unclipped hanger through this opening, and re-attach. Turn cardboard at right angles to one another, making a cross. Center measurements should touch. Tape twisted section of both hangers together tightly.

- Tie the cardboard cross together by looping a 24" piece of colored yarn in both directions until secure. Wind scraps of colored yarn around entire hanger, finishing at the top just above the tape. Tie off the end of each piece of yarn, or secure with glue.

- Cut four stacks of 15 pieces of 4" yarn, each using several colors in each stack. Use one piece from each stack to tie it together in a bundle at the center. Tie again, attaching one bundle to each corner of your mobile.

- Cut four pieces of 12" yarn. Tie one flower circle to each string, and attach other end to one corner of your mobile. It is ready to hang.

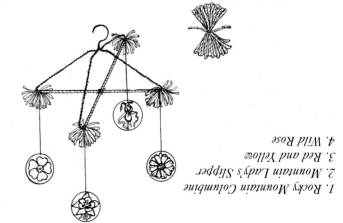

1. *Rocky Mountain Columbine*
2. *Mountain Lady's Slipper*
3. *Red and Yellow*
4. *Wild Rose*

Kids' Spring Recipes

[Adult supervision required]

One healthy way to take care of our bodies and our world is to eat a vegetarian diet, because raising animals for food uses much more of the earth's resources than raising plants for food. It also helps to plan meals that need little or no cooking. As a favor to your planet, try these healthy and tasty vegetarian recipes:

Finger Salads

Clean and cut the following vegetables:

    mushroom caps (remove stems)
    cherry tomatoes (cut in half)
    cucumber rounds
    carrot rounds
    zucchini rounds
    jicama (1/2" cubes)
    celery (1/2" slices)

Using Vegetable Dip as "glue," build your own finger salad using any combination of these vegetables. The only rule is that you must eat one creation before starting another.

Fruit Shake

    1 cup orange or apple juice
    1/4 cup unsalted cashew nuts
    1/4 cup fresh or frozen strawberries
    1 peeled and frozen banana, sliced

Remove lid from blender and pour in fruit juice. Turn blender to puree. While blender is on, add cashew nuts. Next, add berries. Add one banana slice at a time until mixture is thick like a milk shake. Drink while cold.

Vegetable Dip

    1 cup light sour cream
    1 tsp. finely chopped fresh parsley
    1/4 tsp. garlic powder
    1 tsp. nutritional yeast
    1/4 tsp. salt
    dash pepper

Measure all ingredients into small bowl. Stir until well blended.

Breakfast Pizza

    1 whole wheat English muffin
    4 fresh strawberries   OR   1/2 banana
    light cream cheese   peanut butter

Toast English muffin. Spread with layer of cream cheese or peanut butter. Top with sliced fruit. Drizzle with honey to taste.

SUMMER

Red Fox ventures out
    to explore and grow
In golden-green
    meadow grass.
So many things he'll
    need to know
When this fair
    season's past.

Four cygnets waddle and splash and play,
And learn skills as they go,
In the flowing warmth of a waterway
While mother watches them grow.

Summer is nature's classroom. Baby swans, called cygnets, prepare for the challenges of the big world around them. The parent Trumpeter Swans stay alert for danger while they teach their young ones everything they will need to know as adults. Sometimes the cygnets get so curious about all the exciting things around them that they forget their lessons, and parents have to scold. That is part of learning for the swan family.

Wild fruit of summer
        turns purple and red
And hangs from
        branch and vine.
These hungry, wild young
        must all be fed,
And nature invites them
        to dine.

Young raccoons must learn to feed themselves if they
are to survive. They learn by watching and copying their
parents. Abundant food helps them grow stronger and
more confident as they learn how to be independent.

Green grass turns gold
in the glowing sun.
Ripe sweetness fills the air.
Little ones sniff
and taste and run,
Content with nature's fare.

Play time is also learning time. Young Prairie Dogs learn
by playing with parents, brothers and sisters. By playing
they learn social skills as well as develop physical
strength. Every lesson learned now makes the world a
safer place later.

Vacation Sketchbook

Make a book to record drawings of animals, wildflowers and interesting places you see on your vacation. Label each drawing with this information: Who? What? When? Where? Attach a photograph of yourself, the author, to the last page of the book with a glue stick. Write a few sentences about yourself on this page. This is a fun way to remember your vacation and to share it with friends.

Bird Bath

In dry areas, summer is a good time to provide a water source for birds and other wildlife. (You may want to provide water in the winter, too, if natural sources freeze over.) The container does not need to be large or expensive. Trash can lids and plastic trays make good water holders. Put it in an open area where birds have freedom of movement. Dig a hole the same size as your container, and bury it almost up to the rim. Keep water shallow—only one or two inches deep. Place a rock perch in the water and also provide a nearby perch such as a dead branch or a small shrub. Keep water fresh. Watch from a nearby window to see your splashing visitors.

Things to do

Adopt a Park, Playground, or Stream

Your local Parks and Recreation Department may have an organized adoption program. If not, ask for their help in starting one yourself with a group of friends. Set a regular weekly time to clean up litter, paint over graffiti and generally make things more beautiful.

Wear gloves while picking up trash. Ask for adult help with broken glass or anything that looks unsafe. Save aluminum cans, newspapers or other recyclable materials. If you receive money for things you recycle, you may want to find some special way to spend it.

in the Summer...

Pine and Sage Sachet

To make this heart-shaped decoration, you will need:

Three pine needle bundles (use long needled pines with at least 27 needles per bundle)

Two twist ties recycled from the grocery store produce department

One 8" piece of scrap yarn

One small cluster of sage sprigs or wild rosehips

Soak needles overnight in water. After soaking, arrange in three bundles of at least 27 needles each, with center group turned away from the other two. Using a twist tie, bind the three groups together at their bases.

Braid the two groups facing upward, curving each down to attach to the center group with the second twist tie. Twist around each braid as it is finished. Trim center group the same length as braids. You should now have a heart-shaped pine ornament.

With the unused ends of the upper twist tie, attach a small cluster of wild sage.

Fold an 8" piece of colorful yarn in half, and tie it in a knot about one inch from the fold. You will now have a loop in the center of your yarn. Lay yarn on a flat surface with the loop up and the two ends spread to make an upside-down V. Place the heart with the top twist tie over the yarn knot. Bring one side of the yarn through each side of the heart, and tie a bow over the twist tie. Hang this fragrant decoration or give as a gift.

Never pick plants in protected areas, and only pick plants that are plentiful. It is always best to get permission if you are not on your own property.

Butterfly Mobile

• Photocopy the line drawings of butter-flies so that they are 3-3/4" circles. Find

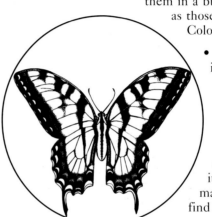

them in a butterfly identification book such as those listed in the Resource section. Color them with felt markers.

• Locate butterfly #1 by finding its name (Tiger Swallowtail) in the identification book.

• Butterfly #2 is orange and black. Find it by looking for its color and shape in the identification book. The next time you see a butterfly, try to remember its colors, shape, size and wing markings. Use that information to find it in the book.

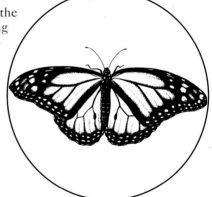

• Follow the instructions for the wildflower mobile (see Spring activities page), using butter-flies instead of flowers. Make four copies of each butterfly, and attach them so that each corner of your mobile has one of each of the two butterflies.

Kids' Summer Recipes

[Adult supervision required]

Sunshine Tea

4 herb tea bags (peach or cinnamon teas are good)
1 gallon water
juice from 1/2 lemon
juice from two oranges
honey or sugar to taste

Place water and tea bags in a one gallon jar. Cover and set out in the sun in the morning. Bring inside in the afternoon. Pour juices into large container. Add tea after removing bags. Sweeten to taste. Serve iced in large glasses.

Fruit Kabobs

You will need one cup of each of the following fruits cut into bite-sized pieces:

fresh pineapple
sliced peaches or nectarines
watermelon chunks
orange slices
fresh cherries or strawberries

On skewers, alternate pieces of fruit until there are at least two pieces of each fruit on each skewer. Eat as dessert or use as an edible stirring stick with glasses of iced Sunshine Tea.

Fourth of July Salad

1 cup blueberries
1 cup strawberries, cut in half
1 cup sliced banana
1 tablespoon sugar
1 cup vanilla yogurt

Place fruit in mixing bowl. Sprinkle with sugar, and mix gently. Stir in yogurt and serve.

Solar Peach Treat

First you will need to make a solar oven. With a glue stick, cover one large sheet of black construction paper with foil, shiny side out. Trim any extra foil with scissors. Roll paper into a large cone with foil on inside by bringing together two corners. Staple to secure. Trim opening until round. Your oven is ready.

In a small, clear glass bowl place:

one peach or nectarine, washed and cut into thin slices

Mix together:

1 tsp. sugar
dash cinnamon
1/2 tsp. wheat germ

Sprinkle over fruit. Cover with clear plastic wrap. Set in full sun inside solar oven for one to one and a half hours. Check at one hour, and adjust so that opening still faces the moving sun. When hot all the way through and sugar has melted, remove plastic, stir and eat.

What other fruit would make a good solar treat?

FALL

Gray Squirrel can
   tell by crispy air
That fall is
      on its way.
She gathers ripe acorns
      to prepare
For a future
      hungry day.

Fall's bright colors scatter and blow
While crops are gathered in.
Each busy creature seems to know
Harsh storms will soon begin.

Fall is nature's harvest time. It is a busy time of year, and those who work hard will be ready for the lean months ahead. Leaves drop, crunchy and colorful, to the ground. Wild crops like acorns and other nuts are ready. Animals like the squirrel and woodpecker must gather and store what they will need to survive the winter.

Wild birds fly south in flocks together
Across a darkened sky.
They visit lands with warmer weather
To find a food supply.

Ducks and geese leave their summer homes to fly south. They eat extra seeds and other foods that will give them energy for many days of flying. Robins, swans, blackbirds, cranes and hummingbirds are just a few of the many birds that migrate to warmer places where there is food during the winter.

Black Bear fattens up
to settle in
As leaves turn
golden-brown,
She finds a place
to make her den
Where an Oak has
fallen down.

Like raccoons and skunks, the Black Bear will
soon spend most of her time sleeping in a
protected place. She often finds a hole under
a fallen tree for a long nap. First she will feast
on acorns and nuts until she is so fat she will
not need to eat all winter.

Things to do

Plant a Tree

Plant a tree or even a grove of trees in your yard, or as a group project, at your school, church or neighborhood park. Ask a local nursery for trees suited to your area that are especially attractive to wildlife.

Some trees that attract wildlife are: Alder, Aspen, Birch, Cedar, Dogwood, Oak, Pine, Sycamore, Wild Cherry and Wild Plum. Ask also for tips on how to plant them so they grow well. Ask a local garden club or nature club if they would like to help sponsor your project. They may donate trees, loan tools or even teach gardening secrets. Trees can also be planted in spring in some areas.

Bird Feeder   [Adult supervision required]

Fall is a good time of year to put up a bird feeder. Fill with bird seed and hang from a tree. Check the Resource section for information on building your own, or make one from a half gallon milk carton using the following pattern. You will need a milk carton, a knife, a nail or ice pick, a ruler, a sharp pencil, two pieces of string each at least 20 inches long and bird seed.

• Two inches from the bottom of the carton, draw a line across the carton on one side. On the same side, draw another line 3" higher. With the knife, cut along both lines.

• Cut up at the corners between the lines to remove a square from the carton side. Turn to the opposite side and repeat.

• Punch two holes in carton top with ice pick or nail. Insert string into each hole. Fill the bottom with bird seed. Your feeder is ready to hang. Tie the two ends together over the tree branch or wherever you want it to hang.

• You can buy bird seed, but you can also save the seeds from your Halloween and Thanksgiving pumpkins. Rinse in a strainer, then lay out to dry on a clean dish towel. Birds also enjoy melon, squash and sunflower seeds. Place your feeder outside a window for hours of viewing fun.

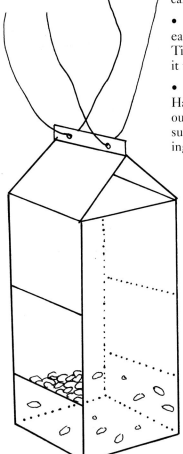

in the Fall...

entative. These people work for you as
em what you would like them to do to
e of your Senator or Representative in
r call the League of Women Voters.

Representative _____
U.S. House of Representatives
Washington, DC 20515

g
tf.
ing
title
cture
lue, or
pocket.
ok? (For
Favorite

Create a Nature Centerpiece

Decorate a table with beautiful things
from nature. Look for things with different
sizes, colors and textures. Consider any of the following:

- Pumpkins
- Gourds
- Dried seed pods
- Indian corn
- Colorful leaves
- Dried grasses
- Pomegranates
- Pine cones
- Interesting branches
- Dried flowers
- Citrus
- Fresh flowers

Start with 3 to 5 pumpkins (depending on the size of your table). Place them on the table near the center. Arrange the other things you have collected around them until you are happy with your design. This is a cheerful way to remind yourself of the bounty of nature. If you include fresh flowers, arrange small vases of water among the other items.

Adopt an Acre of Nature

You can help protect nature's beauty. For example, you could "adopt" a little chunk of rainforest or some beautiful prairie grassland. Write to Adopt an Acre, 1815 N. Lynn Street, Arlington, VA 22209, and ask for information about the Nature Conservancy Adopt an Acre Program. If you would rather adopt an endangered animal, write to Monica Bond, Endangered Species Coordinator, NWF Western Natural Resource Center, 921 SW Morrison, Suite 512, Portland, OR 97205. Ask for information about the Adopt a Species Program.

Kids' Fall Recipes

[Adult supervision required]

Peanut Butter Candy

    1 cup peanut butter
    1/4 cup cocoa
    1/4 cup oat bran
    1/3 cup sugar
    1/3 cup honey
    1 cup chopped, dried apricots
    1 cup chopped, dried cherries
    1 cup finely chopped pecans

Mix first five ingredients in a large bowl. Add fruit, working together with hands. Shape into small balls. Roll in pecans. Store in covered container in refrigerator. Makes 30 to 40 candies.

Vegetarian Bean Soup

    1 can vegetarian refried beans
    1 can (same size) diced stewed tomatoes
    1-1/4 cups vegetarian bouillon (powder or cubes
      with water as instructed on label)
    1 small onion, diced
    1/4 teaspoon garlic powder
    salt to taste

Combine all ingredients in large sauce pan. Simmer for 20 minutes, stirring occasionally. Serve with grated cheddar cheese, light sour cream and corn chips.

Apricot Tasties

    1 cup dried apricots
    4 large milk chocolate candy bars
    1 cup finely chopped pecans

Melt candy over 2 cups water in top of a double boiler. When chocolate is all soft, stir until smooth. Dip each apricot half-way into chocolate, then into pecans. Lay on wax paper to cool.

Fruit Cups

Preheat oven to 350°. In medium baking dish mix:
    1 cup dried apples
    1 cup dried cherries
    1 cup dried apricots or peaches
    2 cups unsweetened apple juice
    1/4 teaspoon cinnamon

Cover and let soak for 15 minutes. Stir again. Cover and bake in 350° oven for 20-30 minutes (until warm throughout). Eat warm, or refrigerate and take a serving in your school lunch. Be sure to put it in a reusable container.

WINTER

The Cedar Waxwing
bounds along
His frosty winter perches.
He hopes for ripe,
red berries on
The branches that
he searches.

Hidden by wind-blown
    drifts of snow
Where limbs hang
    to the ground,
Cottontail has
    a place to go
And safely snuggle down.

In Winter many animals seek a safe shelter where
they take a rest. Days are short and cold. There may
be rain or ice, or perhaps even snow. Bare tree limbs
stretch like skeletons against winter skies. Cottontail
Rabbit depends on her thick fur and the shelter of
low, snow-covered branches to protect her.

Elk gather in the
　　lowland wood
To search for twigs
　　and grass.
They settle wherever
　　food is good
And stay 'til winter's past.

Elk herds travel from mountains to lower elevations
where there is less snow to cover up their food,
which is mostly twigs and grass. Like deer and other
animals who rely on plants for their diet, elk can
have a difficult time moving around and finding
enough food if the snow is very deep.

A Bobcat stalks through falling snows
While searching all around.
She creeps on silent hunter's toes
And never makes a sound.

Bobcat relies on her sharp sense of smell to lead her to her next meal. If she is swift and clever, she will not go hungry, but she must be ready for hidden opportunity. She moves silently and gracefully through a powdery white world. When the snow melts and spring returns, finding a meal will not be so difficult.

Things to do

Decorate a Live Christmas Tree

Decorate a tree in your yard or at your school with edible ornaments for your wild neighbors.

• String unseasoned popcorn, whole peanuts, cranberries and grapes or raisins using a needle and cotton thread.

• Tie wedges of orange to sturdy branches.

• Hang pine cones that have been stuffed with a mixture of one cup peanut butter, one cup corn meal and enough finely ground bread crumbs for easy handling. Roll in bird seed.

• Attach colorful pomegranate halves to branches by tying with heavy string with fruit side facing up. You will have a beautiful tree and lots of happy visitors.

Recycle Christmas Cards

Save cover art and inside verses to make next year's gift tags and cards for special people on your list. Simply cut out designs and glue to pieces of recycled paper that are cut slightly larger than artwork when folded in half. Use a glue stick for neat, clean work. Attach verses to inside or leave blank for your own message.

Christmas Wrap   [Adult supervision required]

To make your own Christmas wrapping bags you will need the following:

> brown paper bags (unprinted)
> paint (water-based)
> small brush
> paring knife
> potato
> ribbon or yarn, red and green

Cut a large potato in half. With knife, carve holly leaf shape on one half of potato. Leaf shape should be raised and surrounding potato surface carved back about 1/2 inch. Do the same with berries on other potato half. Brush red paint on berry stamp. Stamp scattered berries around your sack. Using green paint, repeat the same process with holly leaf stamp. Let dry. Fill your holly wreath sack with a Christmas gift and tie closed with red and green ribbon.

Illustrated Story Book

Materials needed: old Christmas cards, paper, pen or pencil, hole punch, glue stick, colored ribbon or yarn. Create an illustrated story book for someone you love by using several recycled Christmas cards. Spread out at least ten cards to give you a story idea. Imagine what might happen in this story, and rearrange your pictures until they are in the right order for the storybook pages. Cut out the first one and glue it to the first page. Write the beginning of the story on that page. Continue creating pages until your story is finished. With a hole punch, make two holes on the left hand side of each page. Be sure holes match on all pages, one 2-1/2 inches from the top and one 2-1/2 inches from the bottom of the page. Pull ribbon or yarn through both holes and tie on the front side of your book.

Backyard Wildlife Habitat Program

Winter is an ideal time to start planning your own wildlife sanctuary. Send for the National Wildlife Federation's Habitat Package No. 79921 ($18.25). Find out how to get your Backyard Wildlife Habitat Program certificate while bringing all sorts of critters to your yard. Call 800-432-6564 or write to The National Wildlife Federation, 8925 Leesburg Pike, Vienna, VA 22184.

in the Winter...

Native American Rattle

Materials:
> two paper bowls
> transparent tape
> a handful of dried corn or beans
> the cardboard tube from a wire pants hanger
> tempera paint
> 1/2 inch paint brush
> 3 foot piece of cotton, jute or other natural fiber twine
> paper punch or ice pick
> If you have some bird feathers you have collected from nature walks, use those, too.

• Put your bowls together and punch holes about one inch apart around the entire rim. Separate bowls and put corn or beans in one of them (about ten pieces).

• Attach the cardboard tube to rim of this bowl so that it is centered with one end touching top edge and one end hanging over bottom edge like a handle. Tape in place.

• Turn second bowl upside down over first bowl and line up holes. Tape in place using small pieces of tape next to both ends of handle.

• Starting next to the tube, thread the two plates tightly together with the twine. Tie with a firm knot when you have gone all the way around.

• Paint brightly with tempera paints. You may want to paint Native American designs (like the two shown) on each side.

• Wrap bases of three feathers together with tape, insert in end of cardboard tube at edge of bowls at the top of the rattle and tape in place.

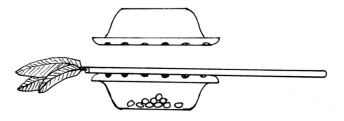

Animal Tracks

It's fun to study animal tracks, which show up well in snow or mud. Go for a walk just after a storm and look for tracks. Who made them? A raccoon? A squirrel? A fox? Or is it the neighbor's dog? Draw the track on a piece of paper. Measure it with a ruler. See if you can find it in an animal track identification book (see Resources). Animal identification books only list wild animals.

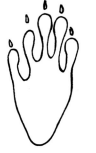

Racoon   *Squirrel*   *Dog*

Kids' Winter Recipes

[Adult supervision required]

Hot Spiced Cider

In a large pan mix:
- 1/2 gallon apple juice
- 1 cinnamon stick
- 3 whole cloves

Place over hot fire just until it comes to a boil. Reduce heat to low, cover and simmer for 1/2 hour. Serve hot in mugs on a chilly winter day.

Cream Cheese Balls

Preheat oven to 350°. Sauté in skillet until vegetables are tender:
- 1 tablespoon butter
- 2 green onions, diced
- 1/4 cup chopped walnuts
- 2 stalks celery, finely diced

Pour into a bowl and add:
- 1 package seasoned dressing mix
- 1 eight oz. package light cream cheese, softened
- 1 egg, lightly beaten
- enough vegetable broth to soften bread (approximately 1 cup)

Mix, adding just enough broth to make bread soft but not soggy. Roll up your sleeves and work everything together with your fingers until completely mixed. Shape into cookie-sized balls and place on cookie sheet about two inches apart. Bake in preheated 350° oven until golden brown (about ten minutes). Eat warm, or take in school lunches.

Spiced Nuts

- 2 tablespoons vegetable oil
- 1 cup raw almonds
- 1 cup raw cashews
- 1 cup raw pecans
- 1 teaspoon garlic salt
- dash of chili powder

Heat oil in large, heavy frying pan for about half a minute. Add nuts, and sauté on medium heat for 3 to 4 minutes. Stir and turn with spatula constantly. Drain nuts on a stack of paper towels, patting to remove oil. Combine garlic salt and chili in large bowl. Add nuts, stirring until they are coated with seasoning. Serve as a snack.

Roasted Pumpkin Seeds

Preheat oven to 325°. Remove seeds from a large pumpkin. Place them in a colander in the sink. Stir with hands as you rinse with water to clean seeds. Place seeds on a clean dish towel and pat dry. In a covered bowl, put pumpkin seeds, 1 tablespoon vegetable oil and 1/2 teaspoon seasoned salt (or more to taste). Cover with lid and shake to season all seeds. Spread on a cookie sheet and roast until golden (about 10 to 20 minutes). Stir once or twice to cook evenly. They are ready to eat hot from the oven.

Notes:

Resources

Books

A Garden For Children, Felicity Bryan, BAS Printers, Ltd.

Adopting a Stream, Steve Yates, University of Washington Press

Animal Tracks and Traces, Kathleen V. Kadlinski, Franklin Watts

Attracting Backyard Wildlife, Bill Merilees, Voyageur Press

Audubon Society Field Guide to North American Birds: Western Region

Audubon Society Field Guide to North American Birds: Eastern Region

Audubon Society Field Guide to North American Butterflies

Audubon Society Field Guide to North American Wild Flowers: Western Region

Audubon Society Field Guide to North American Wild Flowers: Eastern Region

Audubon Society Field Guide to North American Trees: Western Region

Audubon Society Field Guide to North American Trees: Eastern Region
— Alfred A. Knopf, Pub.

Audubon Society Guide to Attracting Birds, Stephen Kress, Charles Scribner's Sons

Bird Feeder Book, Donald and Lillian Stokes, Little, Brown and Company

Butterfly Garden, Mathew Tekulsky, The Harvard Common Press

Child's Organic Garden, Lee Fryer and Leigh Bradford, Acropolis Books Ltd.

Complete Birdhouse Book, Donald and Lillian Stokes, Little, Brown and Company

Complete Outfitting and Source Book for Bird Watching, Michael Scofield, The Great Outdoors Trading Company

Crinkleroot's Book of Animal Tracking, Jim Arnosky, Bradbury Press

Field Guide to Birds East of the Rockies

Field Guide to Western Birds
— Roger Tory Peterson, Houghton Mifflin

Helping Nature Heal, Richard Nilsen, Whole Earth Catalog/Ten Speed Press

Let's Grow! Linda Tilgner, Storey Communications, Inc.

New Green Christmas, Evergreen Alliance, Halo Books

Protecting Our World, Felicity Brooks, Usborne

Simply Vegetarian, Nancy Mair and Susan Rinzler, Dawn Publications

Urban Forestry for Children, Free to teachers, from Cooperative Agriculture Extension, University of California, 4145 Branch Center Road, Sacramento, CA 95827

Vegetarian Sourcebook, Keith Akers, Vegetarian Press

Wildflower Gardener's Guide, Henry W. Art, Garden Way Publishing

Wild Seeds and Plants

Gardening Supplies: C.H. Bacus, 900 Boynton Ave., San Jose, CA 95117. Catalog free

Gardens of the Blue Ridge, P.O. Box 10, Pineola, NC 28662. Catalog $3.00 (refundable)

Holbrook Farm and Nursery, 115 Lance Road, P.O. Box 368, Fletcher, NC 28732. Catalog free

Midwest Wildflowers, PO Box 64, Rockton, IL 61072. Catalog $1.00

Plants of the Southwest, 1812 2nd Street, Santa Fe, NM 87501. Catalog $1.50

Siskiyou Rare Plant Nursery, 2825 Cummings Road, Medford, OR 97501. Catalog $2.00 (refundable)

Wildflower International, Inc., 918 B Interprise Way, Napa, CA 94558 (wholesale)

Gardens Alive! 5100 Schenley Place, Lawrenceburg, IN 47025. Catalog free. Organic gardening supplies, praying mantis, lady beetles, earthworms, bird houses and feeders.

Organizations

National Audubon Society, 645 Pennsylvania Ave: SE, Washington, DC 20009

Sierra Club, 730 Polk St., San Francisco, CA 94109

Global Releaf, American Forestry Association, PO Box 2000, Washington, DC 20013

School Programs

For information about environmental school programs by Diane Iverson and other Dawn Publications authors, call 800-545-7475.

About the Author

Diane Iverson is a grandma who has never outgrown splashing in puddles and climbing trees. Born in California, she now lives with her husband, Doug, in Prescott, Arizona, but you are more likely to find her exploring some wilderness trail. The rest of her time is devoted to sharing her curiosity and enthusiasm with children wherever she visits schools. Children hold a warm place in her heart, and she is probably most happy with a picture book in her hand and a grandchild on her lap.

Acknowledgments

My thanks to the many teachers and students who have shared their ideas and enthusiasm with me over the years, especially Anna Tungseth from Garden Grove, California, School District and the children and teachers of Huntington Beach, California, schools. Thanks to Charles Glen for reviewing the text from a teacher's point of view. Thanks to Dan Montgomery, Jan Hansen and Nina Miller for their valuable support. Special praise goes to my husband, Doug, for his help with photographic research, cooking, doing the dishes and basically keeping the rest of our lives in order. Much thanks to Bob, Glenn, LeeAnn and the rest of the staff at Dawn for giving me the part that was fun, and taking care of the part that was work. Not least important, thanks to Gordon and Gloria for the luxury of time and place, and to Nikko and Autumn for artistic assistance. Blessings on you all!

DAWN Publications is dedicated to inspiring in children a deeper understanding and appreciation for all life on Earth. To order, or for a copy of our catalog, please call 800-545-7475. You may also order, view the catalog, see reviews and much more online at www.dawnpub.com.